Written by **Laura Shiff** • Illustrated by Bev Johnson

What I'm Feeling Is Okay!

A Book about Emotions

Beaver's Pond
PRESS

Edited by Becca Hart
Illustrated by Bev Johnson
Production editor: Hanna Kjeldbjerg

ISBN 13: 978-1-64343-819-1
Library of Congress Catalog Number: 2020915892
Printed in the United States of America
First Printing: 2021
Second Printing: 2021
25 24 23 22 21   6 5 4 3 2

Book design and typesetting by Dan Pitts.

Beaver's Pond Press
939 Seventh Street West
Saint Paul, MN 55102
(952) 829-8818
www.BeaversPondPress.com

To order, visit www.LauraShiff.com. Reseller discounts available.

Contact Laura Shiff at www.LauraShiff.com for school visits, freelance writing projects, and interviews.

For my boys, who make me feel **ALL** the feelings.

—LS

For my family, who has always supported and encouraged me.

—BJ

Right now I'm feeling

happy

as I wake up in my bed.

A big smile is on my face,

and good thoughts are in my head.

I play with all my fire trucks—
they go to save the day!
Right now I'm feeling happy,
and feeling happy
is okay.

Right now I'm feeling

mad.

My face feels hot and sweaty.

Mommy says I have to stop,

it's time to go get ready.

I jump up and I yell,

"No! I just want to play!"

Right now I'm feeling mad,

and feeling mad
is okay.

Right now I'm feeling

sad,

with tears rolling down my face.

I'm really sorry that I threw

my toys across the place.

Mommy gives me one big hug

and wipes my tears away.

Right now I'm feeling sad,

and feeling sad

is okay.

Right now I'm feeling

silly,

as we play chase down the hall.

Mom tickles me and makes me laugh.

Now I'm not sad at all!

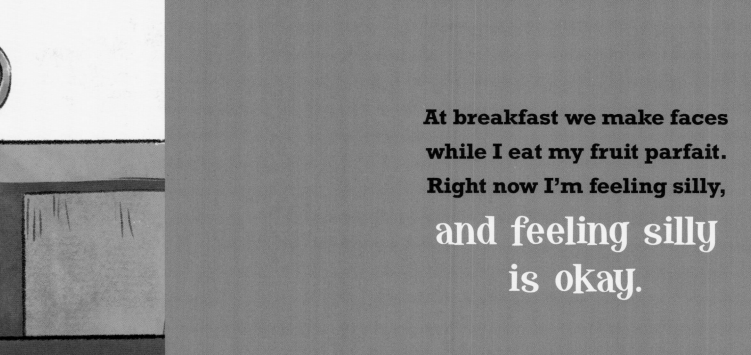

At breakfast we make faces
while I eat my fruit parfait.
Right now I'm feeling silly,

**and feeling silly
is okay.**

Right now I'm feeling

scared.

What was that big, loud sound?

My heart is beating really fast.

Let's go hide underground!

Mommy says it was a thunderclap
that rumbled far away.

Right now I'm feeling scared,

and feeling scared
is okay.

Right now I'm feeling

frustrated–

my Legos will not stick!

When they don't go together,

I want to scream and kick!

Mommy has me take a breath.
She shows me the right way.
Right now I'm feeling frustrated,

and feeling frustrated
is okay.

Right now I'm feeling

worried–

I don't want to go to school.

What if I miss my mommy or

forget a big school rule?

My tummy hurts a little.

I don't even want to play.

Right now I'm feeling worried,

and feeling worried is okay.

Right now I'm feeling

excited!

I want to jump around.
I remembered that today's the day
the fire truck comes to town!

Now I can't wait to go to school.
It will be a real fun day!
Right now I'm feeling excited,

and feeling excited
is okay.

Emotions come,
emotions go,
and all of them belong.
Even when you're sad or mad,
those feelings won't last long.

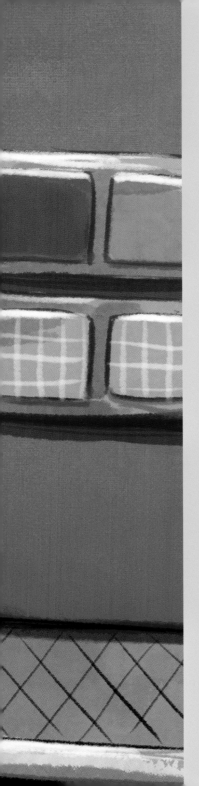

Your feelings are

important,

and they change every day.
You feel emotions all the time,

and your emotions
are okay!

Emotions Scavenger Hunt

Are you ready for a scavenger hunt? Gather a pile of family photos or your kiddo's favorite picture books. Help them identify the emotions in each picture.

Ask them:

- **Why do you think they are feeling that way?**

- **What clues are their faces giving?**

- **What do you think happened to them to make them feel that way?**

- **Using just the emotions in the picture, what stories can you imagine of your own?**

Playing with Our Emotions

Emotions can be big or small, quiet or loud. Here are some fun ways to explore emotions with the little ones in your life.

- Go through the book with your child and identify the different emotions. Ask "What are some things you can do when you feel this emotion?" Create a booklet for them to draw the ideas.

- Grab a mirror. Name different emotions for the child to act out and let the silly faces ensue! Encourage exaggeration.

- Play different types of music and dance out how it makes you both feel.

- On a paper plate or piece of paper, have your kiddo draw a happy face on one side and a sad face on the other. Describe different scenarios and have them flip to how they feel. Some examples include:

  - You can't find your favorite toy

  - We get ice cream!

  - You're playing with a puppy

  - We have to leave the park

- Gather different colors of markers, crayons, or paints and ask your child to illustrate whatever mood they feel.

For classroom-specific curriculum, visit www.LauraShiff.com

About the Author

Laura Shiff has been an elementary school teacher, tutor, daycare worker, and nanny—so she knows a thing or two about children's emotions. She lives in Minneapolis, where she likes to play with her two young sons, go on walks with her Lab puppy, and try new restaurants with her husband. All these boys may drive her cuckoo sometimes, and feeling cuckoo is okay.

About the Illustrator

Bev Johnson is an illustrator and character designer living in California. She loves reading, music, and cats. Drawing makes her the happiest, and feeling happy is okay.